RIA HENNINK

Your child in a different light

Original title: Uw kind in een ander licht
Ria Hennink. Uitgeverij Tourmaline, ISBN 978-3-9524593-0-0

Cover: Ria Hennink
Illustrations: Ria Hennink
Translation: Ria Hennink, Hans Hiltjo Vet
Edited by Sidney Schwartz, New Jersey (USA)

Tourmaline Publisher
www.tourmalineschool.org

ISBN 978-3-9524593-2-4

ISBN 978-3-9524593-2-4

9 783952 459324 >

RIA HENNINK

YOUR CHILD IN
A DIFFERENT LIGHT

Why Your Child Needs a
Spiritual Education

Messages from the Spirit World from
the deceased medium Sita ten Cate to Ria Hennink

With an epilogue of Harrie Salman Ph.D.

Tourmaline

Contents

On wings of light

the child comes to you

and disappears,

into darkness out of sight.

In this darkness is prepared,

what will reappear in light.

***

Introduction

In today's complicated world it is of primary importance to educate our children in spirituality, provided the parents themselves have a spiritual understanding.

This book is designed for parents and educators, who have the education of their children near and dear to their hearts and therefore want to enrich their children's lives with a deep spiritual understanding.

The content of this book is based on messages by my friend, Sita ten Cate (Amsterdam, March 21, 1926 – The Hague, April 8, 2012), who now resides in the world of Spirit. I received these messages from Sita from September 9 until September 27, 2014 about two years after her death.

Sita was a well-known clairvoyant medium during her life. She worked for more than 25 years as a professional medium, giving private sittings, workshops and demonstrations for large audiences. She also led meditation circles and demonstrated her mediumship on radio and television programs. On Sundays, she often conducted worship services for various spiritual associations.

Sita loved flowers. She often gave flower messages during an evening of Spirit messages. The members of the audience brought bouquets of flowers, which were arranged on a table on the stage. Then Sita would select a flower from the different bouquets and arranged these flowers to form a new bouquet. As she did this she gave a message from Spirit to a member of the audience. Sita connected to the Spirit communicator through the flower.

The messages always came with evidence, several pieces of information that definitely proved the identity of the Spirit belonging to the person in the audience. Thus Sita worked to the high standards of English clairvoyants and mediums.

"The Work" as she called it, became the central focus of her life. Often during her demonstrations of mediumship, everyone would receive a personal message from Spirit. Even if there were forty people in the audience, Sita would not stop working until she was certain that she hadn't "missed" anybody.

Several spiritual guides assisted in Sita's mediumship. The most important ones had various cultural and religious backgrounds, during their physical lives. Salomon had been Jewish, Ahmed had been Islamic and Sophie had been Christian. Despite their different religious backgrounds these guides agreed in their messages of love. Sita disliked the earthly bickering and pedantry between different creeds. She considered religion a personal choice, or it just emerged from the culture where one was born. Sita believed "The Great Unknown" had many names.

Sita considered it important to justify herself to "our dear Lord," as she used to call it. She felt a large responsibility for her work and regarded it as a task she had to fulfil to the very best of her abilities. She helped countless people with their most diverse types of problems. However, Sita's greatest satisfaction came when people started to be convinced of a spiritual world and then began to take personal responsibility for their actions.

Sita had a special meditation room in her home where she held a meditation circle until the last few years of her life. Many people discovered and developed a much richer spiritual life in Sita's meditation room.

During her life, Sita wrote two volumes of poems: "Gedichten Gedachten" (Poems Thoughts) was published in September 2007 and "Van dit en van dat" (From This and From That) was published in 2008.

Before I began receiving messages from Sita, she told me I could add suitable material to her texts. She also said the themes of the messages would be familiar to me.

I thank my husband Hans Vet, for all his loving support and advice. He knew Sita since he was twenty-one years old. His decades-long friendship enabled him to provide insightful comments on Sita's work and words, which was extremely helpful during the editing of the original Dutch version of this book.

I am grateful to Harrie Salman for writing the epilogue for this book. Harrie Salman is a Dutch philosopher and a sociologist. He has written many books based on spiritual subjects.

Finally, I would like to express my deepest gratitude to Sidney Schwartz, who edited the English version of this book. Sidney is a medium himself and is the author of several books on spiritual subjects. He lives in the United States and is the Pastor of the Gifts of the Spirit Church in Connecticut and New Jersey.

Ria Hennink   Scharnachtal, Autumn 2016

Sita ten Cate

I The Cosmos and the Human Souls
September 9, 2014

Sita says hello to me each morning and then her messages begin. To put her messages into writing requires intense concentration. Each communication from Sita is four to six hand–written pages. In order not to let the work pile up, I type each communication on the same day that I received it. As I sit down for a communication, Sita is ready and waiting for me to pick up my pen to write on my notepad, which I keep next to my chair.

Sita: you can ask what happens to children when they come to this earth and then find the physical world lacks the spirituality they knew and loved before they were born. They fall into a deep pit of despair when once here on earth they hear nothing about the spiritual world.

They come from our spiritual world, where everyone is surrounded and enwrapped by spiritual beings. Some children see or feel these beings after they are born into the physical world. Therefore, the child misses its spiritual life, when it is lacking in their new physical life. They miss contact with spiritual beings and the proximity of their guardian angels, who helped and supported them in the life before birth. When the child cannot perceive these invisible beings and when the people in his new earthly surroundings are not open to spiritual experiences, then the child cannot recognize it. Suddenly, there is a grievous empty feeling, deep in the child's soul. Often the child has no understanding why this feeling exists.

This caused me to think about my own childhood. I was about eight years old when I had an experience in the garden of the house where we were living. I was alone standing on the lawn

11

next to the house. Suddenly I had this strong thought that I came from somewhere else. I came from a totally different place, one to which I could not return. I never told anyone about this.

Yes, Ria: you knew! You had a memory of your life in the spiritual world, prior to your birth. That is why you could pick up on it, and remember it. When a memory of the spiritual world can be connected to the new experiences of your current life, then much knowledge is gained. Empty mindsets or unprovable beliefs simply fade away when one has real spiritual experiences.

When parents teach a child a simple prayer before bedtime, it supports the child's growing spirituality for the rest of its life. S/He can draw strength from this until the last breath of life. The prayer provides confidence, knowledge, and acceptance of a higher power. To give this spiritual knowledge to a child; that higher spiritual beings protect humans, day and night creates invaluable, unshakable confidence. Years ago prayer was part of a child's upbringing. Unfortunately, in today's world, some people react with disdain or are sceptical about the power of prayer. But dear people: you miss something when you grow up without being able to say a prayer!

The child comes from the Spirit world and through prayer, it once again reconnects with the Spirit world. That is the beginning of a thread with spirit that should never be broken.
When a child learns that s/he has a guardian angel, this also contributes to his/her confidence in life. The old friend, who is already known, is still there.

However, this has to be taught to the child. We are born into this physical life, with a blank slate, we often do not remember much of our life in the Spirit World before our birth. Our parents have to teach us about the existence of the Spirit world from which we just came. Knowledge of the Spirit world strengthens our spirit and provides us confidence to face all the challenges of the physical world. This is what I feel is important today. Do not allow the children to be ignorant of the Spirit world.

You may ask how a child is affected by parents who have no spiritual life. The child has to cope with this fact. It is important parents do not discourage their child when it speaks about memories from the Spirit world, that s/he experienced before this physical life began. It would be most beneficial for parents to write down and save the child's remarks and memories about its life prior to being born, for often times these experiences fade from the child's mind as s/he grows up.

Do not be negative about this subject, for the child will sense the parents' disapproval of this topic. Engage your child in conversation, to discover all you can about what the child remembers, about deceased persons, previous lives, or any other situation you probably will not understand.

I have already explained when the child comes to this earth, bringing its past with him/her. So encourage the child to talk about this topic, and show your interest by asking for further details. In this way, you can learn much from your child. Actually, the adult learns much more from the child, than the child from the parents.

Do not restrict the child's spiritually, but don't impose your spirituality upon your child. For example, it is not necessary for a child to meditate. Let it grow up naturally. Do not force your child to fit a pre-conceived notion. The child often is wiser than we are and everyone has different requirements, since each person brings his/her unique "baggage" from previous lives.

Sing to your child. Expose your child to beauty of life. Rejoice! Have an open heart and be happy that your child came from the

Spirit world to be with you. Your child has come to you with great love: and has chosen you, not anyone else! Receive your child with open arms.

Perhaps your child came to you as an unexpected surprise. Perhaps you feel you are not ready to be a parent, whether it is because you feel there is a lack of money, or that you are not emotionally ready to raise a child. Remember, your child has **chosen** to be born to you. It understands your limitations, and has incarnated to learn through your limitation, and then to develop its spirituality. It is not a stone that suddenly rolls alongside your path. It is a living being: a child migrating from the Spirit world of eternal life. Allow it come in freedom, so that it can freely live.

Does your child come at an inconvenient moment? Bear in mind that we cannot always know what is convenient or inconvenient in our life. We should not ignore our own feelings. However, the Spirit world is always there to assist us; all we need to do is ask. Perhaps we will have to make sacrifices, but is it possible that others made sacrifices for us in a former life? Live an honourable life, so that you can always look into the mirror, and not feel any guilt. Then you can cope with a child that announces itself at an inconvenient moment for you.

The souls here in the Spirit world, who were not allowed to be born are suffering, because they feel unwanted. They have to begin again to build up a new connection. But the unconditional love remains and the child stays in your aura. You do not see through this; that will come later.

Life is Eternal – a constant cycle of descending streams of incarnating souls to the earth and then returning souls of the deceased to the Spirit world. It is a pulsating stream that never stops. It is a mighty scene. I am repeatedly surprised when I see how souls descend in happiness and eagerly want to get to work. How big is their disappointment when they do not succeed in establishing the life they envisioned?

We incarnate to earth with an agenda. We want to fix what we have done wrong. We want to once again be with the people we love. We want to fulfil our destiny, that we established in times long gone. How miraculous is the hustling and bustling of human souls filling the cosmos? They are drawn to return to the earth, just as salmon return to the waters, where their eggs were laid to guarantee offspring. The human being must return to the earth. We still have a long way to go, until thousands of years from now, we evolve into new patterns of incarnation on earth.

Try to imagine the grandiosity of the universe we live in. Think about the wisdom that is hidden in this cosmic development. Let it affect you. Your life is greatly enhanced when you integrate this knowledge. Despite all grief in the physical world, it is a magnificent and majestic place. We can conquer all the sorrow, if we focus on the beauty found in the physical world. When I was on earth I used to think: "Who has invented all this?"

Let life surprise and inspire you. It will renew your life. Isn't that a miracle, by itself? Just think about this.

These are Sita's words. The themes will be repeated in the following chapters of this book. However, each time the theme repeats, Sita highlights them from another point of view.

The following is one of Sita poems, which was recited at my mother's funeral.

The Guardian Angel

I knew you before you came

freshly born as a child to the earth.

I took your hand and helped you stand

and go the long way we call life.

And know I shall not leave you,

even not when all is done.

We go together on a path

of stumbling and standing up.

In God's name once we will

overcome all that is difficult.

After much love and grief

We enter heaven together.

II A Sacred Meeting
September 11, 2014

I have put some flowers on the table today to honour Sita who loved flowers so very much, during her earthly life. Then Sita immediately begins to give me messages. We have been working together each morning for quite some time, and she has provided much information about life after death. Today we again focus on information that will help to guide parents.

Sita: Ria please start writing. I still have more information for you. You were asking whether we could write practical advice for children, or to put it more precisely, for parents and their children. Well, we certainly can do that! One could also consult Rudolf Steiner's work because he established a whole anthroposophical pedagogy about children! This may be advanced for some, but I will try to keep it simple.

Parents can learn much from their children – I have explained this already. Children indeed are very close to the Spirit world. Even after their birth children are still enwrapped in the atmosphere of the Spirit World. Spirit works and communicates with new-born children while they sleep, encouraging their growth, and deepening their spiritual bond. How delicate this new human life is! Adults can feel this.

Just try to focus your attention on the Spirit world surrounding your child, as the child's personality is in the process of development. Try to feel who she or he is and will become. You can begin doing this during the pregnancy. Start keeping a diary and write your feelings and thoughts down. You can begin from the moment you realized that you were pregnant. The development of a child is a wondrous miracle. Inside your

17

body, a human being is growing – a human life. You are privileged not only to witness this but are encouraged to protect and guide this process.

There are invisible changes that occur when you are pregnant. Also people living in the Spirit world come closer to you. You suddenly feel different - more transparent and softer. Your body moulds itself to the shape of the growing child and you can mould spiritually with it. This is a great experience if you are open to it. Sometimes people say to a pregnant woman "enjoy your pregnancy." It is really wonderful when you are able to do so. You can use this special time to work and mould yourself.

Your developing child is coming to you from the other (Spirit) world. There is a whole spiritual component to birth. There is much more involved than merely the male seed connecting with your egg to create a child. That only deals with the physical body. A soul must come from the Spirit world to inhabit the newly formed physical body. Spirit is very involved in this process!

Higher hierarchies, angels, and archangels, *(1) assist the human soul with its descent to the earth; thereafter, this soul connects with both parents. While it is still living in the Spirit world, the soul plans its future for its many years of earthly life. In order to fulfil its planned physical life, the soul has to find a pair of "suitable" parents. Rudolf Steiner fully discusses this subject.

*Rudolf Steiner *(2) speaks about the "pre-birth" life, the preparation of the soul's incarnation and previewing its earthly life. Steiner says that a human being is not born to any parents. In each life the human soul works on the karmic ties. When it returns to the earth for a new life, it will choose to be with people* *with whom it still has unfinished business. For example, a soul may continue working on a project it began in a previous life; however, it may happen in a different way and in a different location. Also, old problems between people are worked on or even solved. Sometimes it may take several lifetimes to resolve certain situations. For spiritual development to occur, "knots" (or problems) from the past must be unravelled. As spiritual evolvement occurs, the soul has less difficulty unravelling knots.*

Sita continues: The descending human soul finds its parents and then connects with the growing life in the mother's womb. This descent does not happen smoothly, because the new connection with a human body limits the possibilities the soul had in the Spirit world. The powers the soul had in the Spirit world are now transformed into physical powers, which make the body, the fruit (foetus) grow. This transformation is a gradual process.

The great miracle of birth is accompanied with many emotions. Birth is a delightful joyful event for those of us living in the physical world. However, it is the opposite for those living in the Spirit world, who find birth a sorrowful goodbye, as the soul leaves its friends and family living in the Spirit World.
In the physical world, the newly arrived child will encounter a full range of emotions: light and dark, warmth and cold. This physical experience is completely different from the soul's experience in the Spirit World; therefore, the child will need to adjust to many new situations.

You as parents are there to help this new human being adjust to its new surroundings. Once you understand all the adjustments your child needs to make, you will be better able to anticipate your child's needs and be better equipped to assist your child in adjusting to the physical world. Now you can appreciate the tremendous differences between the two worlds, and understand how difficult it is to adjust. The child needs to make these difficult adjustments gradually.

Furthermore, you can support your child during your pregnancy. Spiritual beings surround your child, and are also influencing you, helping you bond with the child that is growing within you. During pregnancy your feelings change, as if a sacredness from the cosmos envelops you and your unborn child. This is a very special period in your life. Live in the moment. Be conscious and aware of all these subtle changes. Concentrate on the Spirit world, by giving yourself periods of rest during the day. This quiet time allows you to come very close to the Spirits around you and the child that is growing inside of your body.

*The messages of **Botho Sigwart von Eulenburg** to his family are quite relevant to this topic. He died in 1915, while serving as a soldier in World War I. Shortly after his death, he began to communicate through his sister, who was a medium, and described his life in the Spirit world. He continued giving these messages for nearly thirty years. Some of Sigwart's messages can be found in a book entitled: "Bridge over the River." *(3)*

Sigwart, as I will call him, describes the process a soul must go through, who is about to incarnate into the physical world.

Sigwart explains while it is still living in the Spirit World, the soul that is about to incarnate must attend school. Spiritual teachers or guides assist the soul in creating plans for their upcoming earthly life. The incarnating soul must have a clear strategy, and understanding of the purpose of its new physical life, and what it needs to learn. Sigwart also explains how surprised he sometimes is, when he sees the great enthusiasm and courage some souls have when they decide to lead a physical life full of difficult challenges. This enthusiasm for a new incarnation is necessary, in order for the soul to persevere through the challenges of physical life, for often it is a very lengthy and difficult process for the soul to accomplish its goals.

Sigwart explains that incarnating is like a bath. The spirit waits anxiously, just like a hard working person who longs for cold refreshing water. This desire grows and becomes stronger. Then the spirit looks for its mother who has the task of receiving him. Once this is decided, the incarnating soul does not leave the potential mother anymore, because of fear that something might go wrong. The soul surrounds its potential mother with the utmost care and reverence. Sigwart describes it as follows:

"Then the moment comes when the fruit is ripe. Despite the fact that its desire is very strong, the moment of descent is very radical and perhaps even tragic. It is only in that moment, the spirit realizes that entering into a physical body, means it will be years before it returns to the Spirit world. With a painful cry, it rushes into the stream of "cold water". This frightening transition only lasts a moment and then it concentrates on the mother it has prayed for and surrounds her with boundless love." Sigwart adds: it is very important for pregnant women to know this. *(3)

Parents often do not realize there is already a relationship between themselves and their unborn child. These ties (the knowledge of each other) were already established in the past and will continue to exist in the future.

You can get to know your child before its birth. Take note of all your experiences, and then write them down in a journal. Talk to your child and ask it questions. This will allow you get to know each other and become closer to one another. When the child is finally born and is lying in your arms, you will already have established a strong bond, and will know each other well.

Pregnancy is similar to a journey. One of your dear friends, who lives very far away, informs you that he or she will be coming for a visit. You haven't seen each other for many years, yet you know each other very well.

At last, it is the day of your friend's arrival. You are overjoyed to see your friend and can once again embrace each other. You have looked forward to this moment for a very long time. However, despite your close friendship, you still go through a period of adjustment, of getting used to being with each other again.

By talking to and bonding with your baby, while it is still inside of you, you shorten the awkwardness of the first meeting, and getting used to each is a much shorter process.

*Rudolf Steiner wrote affirmations that can be said during pregnancy and after the baby's birth. *(4)*

Before birth:

*And the soul of the child,
Be it given to me
According to Thy will
Out of the worlds of the spirit.*

After birth:

*And the soul of the child,
Be it guided by me
According to Thy will
Into the worlds of the spirit.*

Also be aware of the changes around you: within yourself, of the world and in the cosmos. Ask your guardian angel for strength. A cosmic event takes place, in you, and with you, and you are privileged to be a witness of it. Every individual incarnating to earth is a cosmic event. The new-born individual comes from the great eternal cosmos to earth in order to work on advancing its spiritual development. This principle holds true, whether the child lives in the rich man's mansion, or in the garbage dumps of a city's slum. We all want to live on this earth; we want to grow and work for the future. Parents support the newly arrived soul. Everyone has a turn to descend to a new life on earth. Be aware of this when you are busy with your notes in your new baby diary. You can learn much, especially during the pregnancy, because then you are open to the world "above." It is just a miracle.

You see we have a nice start. This information is important for the young people who will soon become parents. They will have to learn that birth is a process, where heaven and earth come very close. If they are open to it, they can have extremely powerful experiences.

Tomorrow we continue and discuss the arrival of new, holy life on earth.

1) An archangel is a spiritual being who guides the people of a nation. Angels guide individual human beings.
2) Man's Being, His Destiny and World-Evolution
   Man's Being: Lecture II (GA 226)
3) Bridge over the river, translated by Joseph Wetzel, Steiner Books, 1974, ISBN 978091014259
4) http://wn.rsarchive.org/Articles/Prayers/Prayrs_a01.html

Sigwart

III The Birth and the Time Afterwards
September 12, 2014

Immediately, I had a clairvoyant vision, as I sat down to begin my communication with Sita. I clearly saw Sita welcoming me into her house. She directed me to the sitting room, where her favourite green chair is waiting. It is exactly like the visits we used to have when Sita was still alive.

Sita: As soon as a baby is born, the baby's connection with the Spirit world slowly begins to fade. This gradual process begins as the soul descends into the physical body. Now the baby has to conform and adapt to its new body, which we will call "an instrument," because that is what it actually is. The child will experience more and more of the limitations of the physical body, but in the end that will not be a problem, as the child slowly learns how to use its new physical body.

As the child tastes its first mouthful of milk, it becomes an inhabitant of the planet earth. Until that moment no external nourishment was needed because it did not drink while it lived in its mother's womb. However, after its birth, the child becomes an inhabitant of the planet earth and has to learn to sit, crawl, walk and talk. Angels also help the child during this transitional period. The child uses the spiritual powers it still possesses for further formation and growth of its body. Now the brain begins to function, and the child will discover its thinking process. The parents can observe how their child learns, as it begins to adapt itself to various earthly conditions.

Mothers and fathers: look at your child! Feel how the atmosphere that surrounds the child changes every day. Describe what you feel. How does the space surrounding your child feel? Do not take pictures using your camera's flash, exposing your child to the fierce harshness of the intense light. Do not immediately harden it. Especially during those first days of your child's life, you should try to feel the baby's needs. Let it feel free, without being groped at from all sides. How would you react to this lack of freedom?

Let the baby develop. Just give it time to adjust to its arrival here on earth. Provide your child warmth, a daily rhythm, and above all love -- endless love. The child gave you its love by being born to you. Just imagine you were a baby once again. How would you feel to be so very tiny and vulnerable? Who would you pick to be your parents? Where do you belong? A child can unfold and fully develop in surroundings full of love, and with warmth that comes from the heart. During the coming years, it has to outgrow all the limitations of being a child living under earthly conditions and to get accustomed to this specific situation. The child is constantly learning, and coping with many new situations. However, to develop freely doesn't mean without rules or limitations. Every developing child has to learn where its limits and boundaries are.

Protection: We never would allow a small child to go near a hot stove, where it could burn itself. We protect a baby against outside, strange influences. First, it has to get used to its own quiet surroundings -- in the house in which it will live. Do not create any unnecessary stress or turbulence near your baby, because your baby is very sensitive. It is aware of everything that happens around it. Your unrest becomes the restlessness of your child. Your fears become fears of your child. For nine months your baby was extremely close to you; it knows you extremely well; and absorbs your love, your fears, and your vulnerability. For a successful future, the child needs to become self-confident, and have trust in itself and others. The child must grow into an adult who can live independently and without fear.

It is "a crime" that many countries mandate children must go to school at a very young age, because they have not yet been able to build up enough confidence in their own surroundings. It can also be their confidence to be left alone is not fully developed. Try to become sensitive and aware of your child's feelings. Do not ask it too many questions, but try to feel what your child is feeling. Children may feel too much pressure because they are not ready to answer too many questions.

It is much better for the child to ask you questions. Leave it in peace. What I mean is: keep it very simple. Help it on its way. Do not overload your child with things it doesn't understand. Don't overwhelm by cramming loads of toys into your child's bedroom. The child has to focus -- develop its attention and learn to concentrate. This focus should begin at a very early age. Try to feel when your child is overloaded and overstimulated by external objects. You as an adult could not handle this overstimulation; it would drive you crazy. It would be like your cupboards being so stuffed with items that you wouldn't be able to find anything. It is the same for your child.

It is very easy to teach a child to love nature. Go outside as often as you can, whether it is to the woods, a park, a lake or anywhere else in nature. Teach your child to listen to the sound of birds, which is healthier for your baby than sounds coming from a television or a telephone.

Monitor your child's exposure to the world. Only allow age-appropriate stimulation. Computers, television, tablets and other devices will only bring chaos into your child's daily life, if your child is exposed to them before it has the capacity to handle them. These devices will create restlessness and confusion in the soul of a new human being. Rest, space, and order are important to your new-born child. Also do not forget tenderness, which is very important. The feelings your child experiences in the beginning of its life will become the repertoire for the rest of its life. When it does not experience the feelings of love, tenderness, and attention as an infant, then your child will grow up having difficulty in developing and accepting these feelings. The first seven years of life are of the utmost importance. Therefore, open yourself to the world of Spirit and ask your child's guides for help, in specific situations, and whenever you have difficulties.

We receive most of our information from modern media. Every now and then stop this flow and listen to your own heart. Feel how you experience this. What is needed, in order to allow your child to grow up to be an independent human being, who feels responsible for his deeds? Listen to your own angels. Assist your child in finishing his task, or in the future when the child has become an adult, and s/he is equipped to live independently from you. One day you will have to let go of this new being, who is now lying in your lap.

Then you need to have substantial confidence in yourself, so that your child can mirror you, and can accomplish its desires in an unknown future. Look into the future with the fullest confidence knowing your child – just as yourself – will always be guided by Spirit.

Therefore, say an evening prayer, even if you say it hesitantly and softly, while your child lies in its bed. This will invoke trust and tranquillity for both you and your baby.

The prayer combines the beautiful rhythm of the inspired words with the healing cosmic energy. That will nourish the child's soul, and will give it an inner hold. So before your child goes to sleep at night you create a very special moment together with your child. You do not have to wait until your child can understand the meaning of the prayer's words. It also works without this understanding, as it is the whole atmosphere and the power, which emanates from the words of the prayer, that will have an effect on both parent and child. You will see that you learn many things from and with your child. Make your child the central part of your life by giving it love, love, love.

Rudolf Steiner says it is important for a child to learn to pray. If the child doesn't learn to pray, he or she will not possess the ability to work in a healing way through the spoken word, when it is older.

If we teach a child to pray — if, that is, we teach him to develop a prayerful mood and feeling, the effect of it will swing back into his life after many years. It swings back in the interval, but then swings out again further, and only later, after a very long time, does the feeling of prayer come back and manifest in a mood of blessing. As I have often said: No-one will be able in old age to bestow blessing upon others, merely from his presence, from the imponderable elements in his nature, if in childhood he has not learned to pray. Prayer turns into the power to bless. That is how things come back in life.*(1)

1)   The Mission of the Archangel Michael, The Revelation of the Secrets of Mans Being, By Rudolf Steiner, lecture December 6, 1919 in Dornach, Bn 194.1 and 174a, GA 194 and 174a (English text published in the Golden Blade, 1984)

Here is an evening prayer for very young children. In Chapter 11 you will find a shorter prayer.

My heart is grateful
that my eye may see
that my ear may hear
and that I may feel clearly
in mother and in father
in all dear people
in stars and in clouds
God's light
God's love
God's presence.
They will as I sleep
protect me merciful
in light
in love

30

IV The Small Child

September 13, 2014

My life is very busy at this time, yet I still dedicate time each day to working with Sita. Loyal as she is, she keeps coming each morning and immediately begins communicating with me.

Sita: Today I want to discuss kindergarten age children. As you know I have a lot of experience with them.

Sita was a mother, but she also was a kindergarten teacher. Thus she speaks from much experience in dealing with children of this specific age.

The young child of kindergarten age is very influenced by its surroundings; since it is still in a phase of discovery. Anything can make an impression on the child. This daily stimulation can have a chaotic effect on the child since it wants to absorb everything. Give your child time. It is not necessary that your child has to do everything or is able to do everything. It is not necessary that your child can read when entering kindergarten. Unfortunately, the classrooms, as well as the exterior of many schools are often poorly decorated; which doesn't stimulate the child very well. Allow your child to play and discover its world!

Grant your child those first few years of freedom without formal schooling, without obligations; without defensive armour. Let your child enjoy freedom for as much time as possible! "Some people claim that school is good for developing "social contacts," but social contacts will develop automatically when your child interacts with friends, brothers, and sisters or plays with other children on the playground.

Just look what your child has to encounter in life. Life is much more complex than when I was a child on the earth plane. Therefore, it is important for you to monitor your child's feelings.

Let your child develop in a natural way. Most children do not need to be monitored the entire day. Let them play naturally, without electrical appliances, which restrain the child's development and concentration. Especially now that society is so focused on materialism, it is very important that your child develops a love for nature. The best way to accomplish this is to be a good example! Resist the urge for continuous use of a mobile phone, computer or any kind of electronic device. These devices keep you away from real life. Especially the young child, who constantly absorbs information, should not be overstimulated by these devices. Wait as long as possible to bring your child into contact with the virtual world.

Synthetic fabrics should also be avoided. The young child feels better in natural materials, this includes clothing as well as its toys and environment. The full effect of synthetics and chemical substances within clothes and toys is not fully known yet, but certainly, it will not be without any harmful consequences.

Pay attention to your child's nutrition, just as you pay attention to your own. When you want to ensure the best for your child's future life, then a healthy start is of the utmost importance.

Maintain praying before bedtime. Think about how to teach your child to appreciate and be grateful for its daily food. Teach your child that foods do not come from a factory or even the market, but from the plants in the field. Without bees and other insects, we would have no food. Your child should learn about this as soon as possible. This is the starting point for a healthy nutrition and way of life. To show gratefulness and respect to the earth and cosmos sets the right accent. The Cosmos and the earth nurture the crops in the fields and subsequently provide us with our food.

A healthy start with the food pattern of your child forms the basis for a healthier life as an adult. Your child will follow your example. Just look at what you eat as an adult! Often the foods you eat are based on the patterns of what your parents ate. We often cook the same food and meals as our parents.

If your child grows up constantly eating fast food, then at a later age it will be very difficult for your child to change to a healthy nutritional pattern. It is the same with spirituality.
Show respect for your daily food; for the vegetables from the garden or from the market. Plant some herbs or vegetables for a salad. This is even possible to do on a balcony of an urban apartment. A child learns from seeing and feeling. By observing the growing of food, the child will connect to the oneness of the cosmos.

Technology is a tool and is not essential for our existence. Try to keep technology out of reach of your children for as long as possible. By doing so your child will be able to stay in contact with the Spirit world much longer. Contact with the Spirit world dissipates through abundant and bad impressions. That is why it is also important your child gets sufficient rest and sleep.

Give as much structure as possible to your own life and that of your child. Make sure you and your child get plenty of rest. Leave your mobile phone at home, so you won't be distracted all the time. Enjoy spending your time being together with your child! The time you have to enjoy your child's childhood is very short. Be close to your child and feel the Spirit world around it during the quiet moments. Keep your impressions to yourself and do not tell your child what you are sensing. These are your own experiences, and there is no need to share them with your child.

Your child feels what you feel, so try to raise it without the dark clouds of worries that may disturb you. You are your child's educator. Your child is not your therapist or your helpline. Do not discuss your worries with your children. This also applies to older children. They do not have the capacity to handle this burden and they will feel responsible for your problems. This will hamper their own development. Therefore, keep your child free from worries and trouble for as long as possible. Pray for your child and for yourself and ask for the best possible protection from the Spirit World.

*Sigwart says: "Pray a lot; that always forms a helping ring consisting of waves of common frequency that will keep bad influences away from you." (Beginning of May 1916) *(1)*

1)   Bridge over the river, translated by Joseph Wetzel, Steiner Books, 1974, ISBN 978091014259

V Becoming Aware
September 15, 2014

I have felt Sita's presence in the past few days. I saw her hand with her familiar golden ring with a yellow stone mounted on it. Most of the time she begins her messages immediately after I sense her. It is important that I sit properly in order to be as relaxed as possible when I write. Often the text is long, and sometimes my hand hurts from writing for such a long time.

Sita: As the child grows, it is extremely important the parent observes its child, to be able to guide, steer, and support the child. "Growing up automatically" which happened in the old days, is no longer possible. Today's surroundings have been *forced*. Parents have to understand those surroundings, and they have to anticipate what is coming and have to anticipate the effect upon the child.

Sita speaks of a world or surroundings that have been forced. This means that it has become particularly difficult to isolate the children from the surrounding world, i.e. the internet, television and social media. It is almost impossible to stop children from accessing them.

Awareness is the answer here. Also being aware of your own life. What do you stand for? How independent are you? How are you influenced by your surrounding world and culture? How much do you comply to cultural influence? How much do you resist that influence? To what extent are you a free thinker?

You will gain much insight by answering these questions, which allows you to become a better example to the world and your child. Then you can guide it through the jungle of entanglements, which often entrap people.

For example, feel the effect different types of music has upon you. There are many types of music that enrich and inspire the human soul; however, there is also music that brings disharmony and has destructive power on the soul.
I call this destructive music "soldiers music" for it bring the gloominess of doom to human consciousness. Be aware of this and listen to music that will have a positive effect upon you and your child.

Nowadays it is important to see through the effects of the culture of doom, which is everywhere today. That is why it is so important to do positive, and constructive activities to counteract the pervasive negativity of the culture of doom.
The battle between this positivity and negativity is on earth, and the future of the human race is at stake. The people who are currently reincarnating will fully meet and experience this struggle.

"Yes", you can say, "this struggle has always existed. Just look at the Second World War and the many other wars on this planet". However, I do not speak about those physical wars. The war I am describing is the fight for the human soul.
Humankind must focus on the light, otherwise, humanity will not continue. The darkness that is so prevalent today has to be recognized and then rejected so it will not penetrate your heart, where it has the potential to do much damage.

Otherwise fear will overwhelm the people and before they are aware of it, they are no longer able to escape it. Young people are very impressionable and can easily succumb to the darkness. Often this darkness is not recognizable at first because initially, it has a mysterious and irresistible quality that is attractive to young people. However, soon afterwards, they become trapped and then they can no longer move back into the light. Drug usage is a perfect example of this.

Humanity has to recognize what is good for the human soul and what leads the soul into darkness. It is imperative for parents to create a positive desire for the good of their children.

Learn to know your own limits! Ask for advice when you need help. Seek support from people who strive for the same positivity as you. Then you will find the support you need to wage this battle against the darkness and the negativity of the virtual world. This will help ensure healthy positivity for your child.

Look for the positive surroundings for your child to grow. The home is the basic starting point. Make it a warm safe haven for your child! Attention and love build the positive stability of being together. That makes it easier for your child to deal with new situations and strengthens the goodness within your child. This is the easiest way to be the best parent to your child: give your child attention and love! This is the most powerful tool to block negative influences from penetrating your child's direct environment.

You can utilize the principles of old values and traditions, but you may "translate" them into a modern way. These principles will help you. Just teach them to your child in a positive and "playful" way. Dogmas do not help nowadays. You can use poems and of course you can live the principles of the Ten Commandments. Then you are modelling the basic principles which help form a decent human society.

The Ten Commandments can still be relevant, especially when they are translated to modern times and viewed in a modern way. When we are aware of a higher world, we then feel a responsibility towards both the higher world and with life on earth. This becomes a new compass to guide us in our lives, then we take another step towards a healthier society and a better future.

Nowadays it is more and more apparent that lying has become normal. This is a violation of trust and is full of deceit; which is very destructive to society. Unfortunately, deceit is creeping into all aspects of our society. It is of the greatest importance to be aware of this destructive force, so you can teach your child from a very young age: **speak the truth**! It is as simple is that! However, putting this into practice is not always as easy as you may think. You may have to repeat and reteach this to your child more than once. Always remember: you are the example! You, as the parent, provides the example for your child. You show it how to live. When you are faithful to the truth, then your child will absorb this and will internalize this value. It all begins with you!

VI Respect and Esteem
September 17, 2014

Sita informs me that she once again is "passing by" to bring new messages. I clearly feel her strong energy.

Sita: Today we are dealing with the subjects of respect and esteem. These are very important in life. Respect and esteem are no longer taught to children; people do not recognize them any longer. Respect and esteem have become trivial, are downplayed, and are treated scornfully. One should be aware of this. Parents need to impart respect and admiration when they are educating their children. Always speak with respect about other people, never use injurious language or disdain. You should not speak these negative words.

Be aware of your speech and of what you say about others. Do not judge other people. Teach your child not to condemn and judge anything or anyone. Everyone is in a different location along his or her evolutionary path. No one is of lesser value, because of his or her social status or profession. It is of the greatest importance to remember this. Condemn no one in the presence of your child!

Your child will model and repeat your behaviour. If you criticise your child in a particular situation, you will be setting an example for your child to repeat this behaviour when a similar situation occurs in the future. You want to be a positive role model, not a negative one. Refrain from all judgement and negativity.

Steiner indicates how important respect and esteem are in the development of mankind.

"He who knows such feelings of respect and devotion in a natural way, or who got them implanted by a right education, brings a lot along with him, when in his later life he seeks an entrance to higher knowledge. He who doesn't bring such a preparation, meets with difficulties at the first steps on his path to knowledge, if he doesn't cultivate a feeling of devotion with all his force."
*Rudolf Steiner further indicates how in our civilization people are very inclined to criticism: to judging and condemning. *(1)*

Be aware of your own behaviour. Your behaviour must be pure. When it sometimes isn't, be sure to correct it. This provides an excellent example to your child. Human beings are not perfect. When your child sees that you correct yourself, it will be imprinted by this example.

Young children should be taught to respect their elders and their teachers. This is a correct attitude. Children need examples, to model their own behaviour. They need goals to strive for.

We need to see and accept that another person is further along in his/her spiritual development. However, that is no reason to become envious or jealous. Those emotions have no place in a spiritually evolved person. Learn to be objective! Be aware that you can learn much from your fellow human beings. Everyone has past lives and everyone's experiences are different. Astonishment and admiration about this great human mystery are appropriate attitudes. By living with these values, your child and others around you will begin to experience this through your example.

Look at your own past. Did you look up to your parents as an example of how they were dealing with life? You were taught respect and admiration. "Honour your father and your mother." That is how we used to grow up and that is also a good foundation for young people, who still have a lot to learn in life.

A sudden desire for spiritual growth manifests when one is older and approaching the end of one's life's journey. If one grew up without feeling respect and admiration, one may feel blocked on how to develop spiritually. It is important for people to realize that one continuously grows and develops during one's lifetime. Feeling that one already knows everything is a dangerous block to spiritual evolution and is a burden for one's surroundings. Live your life in curiosity; question where we come from and where we will go. This will make your life a thrilling adventure, filled with surprising discoveries. A thirst for knowledge is the path to advance your spirituality! And you can be your child's tour guide along this exciting path.

1) How to know Higher Worlds, A Modern Path of Initiation, GA 10

Rudolf Steiner

VII Nourishment for the Soul
September 19, 2014

Sita starts immediately. She approaches her work enthusiastically, just as she did when she lived on earth.

Sita: Of course you will give your child healthy food. This will not only provide your child a stronger body but also the possibility for stronger spiritual development. You must have good nutrition to accomplish this. You can find that in Rudolf Steiner's work. *(1)

Thus you can give your child a good start in life, by providing your child with a balanced diet. This is important for yourself as well. Nowadays we have a greater understanding about what effect specific substances have on the human body. However, these substances also affect the spirit as well. Today, we have greater knowledge about the effect of sugar has on the body, and that many aches and pains are caused because of the wrong diet. Therefore, "everything in moderation" is the best advice. Choose the correct diet for yourself and your family, in order to bring balance and harmony into both your body and spirit.

Much has been written documenting excessive sugar and fat in the diet leads to obesity, tooth decay, and causes many other discomforts.

Food for the soul is needed as much as the daily portion of vitamins and minerals. Your child comes from the Spirit world to this earth with certain tasks to fulfil in this new life. You can support and encourage your child to develop his/her spirituality. Otherwise, the world is empty for the child's soul.

43

In order to live and to survive as human beings, we need support from the Cosmos.

The evening prayer keeps your child's connection to the Spirit world intact. You can help your child to have a stronger connection through religious education. Don't be afraid. You do not have to belong to a traditional church to develop your child's spirituality. Yet, in some situations a good spiritual church leader has much to offer; especially if his mind is open to the spiritual content of the doctrine rather than strict dogma.

Sita was a very religious person; however, without being a member of any particular church. She was open to all religions and other people's beliefs. She lived many years in Islamic countries. She had different guides from the Spirit world, who inspired her work. Her most important guides were Salomon, Ahmed, and Sophie – respectively originating from the Jewish, Islamic and Christian cultures. In spite of their different religious backgrounds these guides agreed in their messages of love. Sita did not like the earthly bickering between different religions. She considered religion a personal choice or you belonged to the religion associated with the culture of your birth. The great unknown had many names for her. That is why I like to add that every religion can be a good spiritual shepherd, and has a lot to offer.

But the main thing is that you develop a sincere and honest relationship with the Spirit world, which becomes central to your life. It is important to trust in Spirit and make yourself available to the help from the Spirit world, that is always available to you. We do not have to cope with life alone. Sometimes we may feel alone, but we are NEVER alone! When you have that knowledge and confidence and then teach it to your children, they will receive the fundamental foundation for their soul's life, which will be priceless for the rest of their life.

During one's lifetime one often is faced with the most difficult and seemingly hopeless situations. Your child has to be given spiritual confidence so that s/he will never lose courage in any difficult situation. In the first place, your child needs to understand that difficult situations have a purpose. Everything happens for a reason. Those difficult times are in one's life as a test; to overcome the difficulty effectively and with help from the Spirit world. One's guardian angel is the first source of help. Do not be concerned that you don't have one. All human beings have a guardian angel, who watches them. To contact your guardian angel, all you have to do is to send out a prayer.

In the past, all this was a lot easier because people still believed in the Father, the Son and the Holy Ghost. Prayer was a fixed element during the day, even if it was only the prayer before dinner. The presence of God in life was not doubted. People "automatically" prayed when they were in need. That is where people directed themselves: to God; to Christ. Today some people still pray. God did not abandon humanity, but humanity abandoned God. Therefore, much disconsolateness has come into human existence. The souls have become dry, without any source of nourishment, because so many people do not know how to find God or Christ. They have ignored that spiritual connection for so long during their lives. Without a connection to God, humanity loses hope, loses confidence, and becomes lost. The food which feeds the soul is faith, hope, and love. Humans need these as much as they need daily bread.

Therefore, think about what you want to teach to your child. Which food will be in your child's daily diet? And does this diet also contain spiritual food for your child's soul? For your child requires both so it can become a complete human being, which lives as well on earth as in the Cosmos. We have to be aware of the fact that we all are cosmic beings, who live in eternity. For that path into eternity, we need knowledge and insight:

knowing about the eternal; about the huge cosmos and the development of men and their shepherds.

The shepherds of men protect us in love. They surround us with their care and attention. Let us from our side strive to an inner conviction, like mankind had in the past. Then we can enter the future with the fullest confidence and peace of mind. When you have this within yourself, then you can provide a good foundation to give to your child. Nowadays we can see everywhere that souls are not nourished; they become dry and wither. This is the result when faith, hope and love have been abandoned.

Tomorrow we will continue this topic because I need to explain even more about the food for the soul. The Creator provides these abundant thoughts for humanity.

1) In several lectures Rudolf Steiner spoke about nutrition: GA 57/96/347/350/352/354/351

VIII Gratitude

September 20, 2014

Ria I am here. We will continue our story. All human beings need to have thankfulness as part of their lives. Therefore, that's the subject I wanted to continue from yesterday; however, yesterday is now. Time does not exist. All things happen at the same moment, in the now.

Sita often spoke and wrote about "time." During her last years, the subject of all her New Year wishes were poems about "time."

Sita: When gratitude is absent from our lives, we will not see the light approaching us. How can we accept someone's feelings of gratitude, when we don't recognize that feeling? Be grateful for your health: that you live every day without pain. Be grateful that you see the sunrise. Be grateful that you have enough food on your table. Be grateful that you are not alone or lonely; that you have a child. There is a multitude of other things for which to be grateful!

Every day when you become aware of something for which you are grateful, write it down and meditate on it. Then after one month review your list of all the things for which you were grateful. You will be surprised when you realize you have so much to be thankful for. Then continue this project for another month.

When you pay attention to all things for which you are grateful, you will find new things will be put on your list. For example, a friend calls, just when you needed help; or the sun begins to shine just at the moment you are discouraged, sitting in a corner pondering about all that has gone wrong in your life. And so on and so on.

Your child will be better able to appreciate its life and will develop a positive feeling about the meaning of life when it is familiar with gratitude. Learning to be grateful towards the creation and to its fellow human beings is very important. Natural satisfaction is linked to thankfulness. When a human being is satisfied, then happiness is part of its life. How much happier are you, when you are satisfied? When you can be satisfied with your own life and with your surroundings, then once again there is something for which to be grateful.

Both qualities of gratitude and satisfaction are of great benefit to the human health. Ungratefulness and discontentedness are germs for diseases. It begins in your spirit then the illness manifests in the physical body. Just think about that concept: the origin of diseases that destroys our health lies in our soul. Therefore, a satisfied person is a healthy person!

Gratitude and satisfaction have a positive effect on socializing with other people. People like to come into contact with a grateful person, for the grateful person transmits light and power to his surroundings. By emanating gratitude and satisfaction, we create a healthy situation for society. Our own behaviour influences our neighbours. This is also applicable for your family. Teach your child these qualities through your own attitude and behaviour. Thus you can remove many sources of sorrow and disappointment in life. For there is always something to be grateful for or to be satisfied with. Let these feelings triumph over any setbacks in life.

Your child needs to be able to deal with setbacks in life. The more tools like gratitude and satisfaction it has learned during its youth, the better able it will be to handle the storms in life. Educate yourself and be aware of your own strengths and positive attitude. Your soul already possesses these qualities you just have to emanate them. Your child will grow and flourish by seeing your positive example. For life is full of difficult challenges, and we have to find the strength to forge through them, and not be defeated by discontent and despondency.

Thanks for the light that shines every day
Thanks for the flowers, that pamper our eyes
Thanks for the bird, that sings to us
Thanks to the Creator, by Whom all exists.

Autumn is the time when the crops are being gathered and processed. Since the beginning of time, autumn has been the season of thankfulness for abundant crops; and many cultures still celebrate Thanksgiving-feasts. A successful crop was not taken for granted because drought could easily prevent crops from growing. Nowadays mankind should remember this, and be sincerely grateful for a plentiful supply of food. This gratitude should also be expressed during meals, when a prayer or grace is said or when a short moment of silence is held.

Nothing should be taken for granted, especially dealing with our supply of food. Much physical work was done for the crops to be harvested. However; the cosmos also provided a lot of energy that allowed the crops to grow. With this in mind, we as human beings must take time to express our appreciation for our food. It is our task to teach this appreciation to our children. When they have this appreciation, they can share it with other children, then there will be a more prevalent understanding of how the cosmos nurtures humanity, by providing humanity with its daily bread.

Life on earth and in the cosmos is an inscrutable mystery. Humanity was assigned a role in this mighty process of creation, which obliges us to be thankful towards the Creator.

Poor sheep we are, when we do not know our good Shepherd. We will be lost, when we do not hear His calling.

IX Courage and Tolerance
September 22, 2014

As I sit quietly in my chair, I find myself in a very beautiful atmosphere knowing that Sita still has more information to share with me.

Sita: Dear people; even young people have knowledge of life. They understand that challenging situations arise during one's lifetime. In order to face those challenges, one needs much courage.

Perhaps you don't always realise this, but hidden deep inside yourself exists a source of courage, that you have brought with you from former lives. You need to bravely face difficult circumstances and be fully confident. This can help you, even if it is just during your visit to the dentist.

Through such challenging situations, whether they are large or small scale, provide us the opportunity to use our courage. We all need these challenges because they provide us with opportunities to grow. As we develop a courageous attitude, it increases our self-confidence. Then, when even larger challenges occur, we are better equipped to handle them, since we have more courageous energy and are therefore more powerful to deal with the situation.

As we face our challenges with courage, we serve as an example to our children. The only way to teach courage is by our example. Encourage your child to be self-confident. Life is actually a school for us to grow and spiritually evolve. Therefore, every experience that increases your child's confidence is increasing its courage, and eventually, when your child has grown into an adult, it will have the tools to explore every path in life. Trust your child will be able to accomplish what it has set out to do, and know that Spirit supports both you and your child.

For many children, the first school day is challenging. Do not dismiss any fears your child may have. Never ridicule a child who is fearful. Such ridicule destroys self-confidence. Instead encourage and support your child. Help it to face its fears. Help it rise when it has fallen. This love will develop courage and confidence in your child, when it was lacking. Life is a process of rising and falling, which does not change until your last breath. Thus until the moment, when you transition back to the Spirit world, courage and that confidence are indispensable.

Be tolerant when your child does not behave exactly as you want it to. When its behaviour is bad, talk to your child about it, but always in a way that rejects its behaviour, but not the child itself. Teach your child to be tolerant.

It seems that everything today has to be instant, but that is not always possible in daily life. Teach your child patience, because not all things can be done instantly, some things need time. Just accept when your child needs more time to learn a particular task. Have the courage to be tolerant.

Many people are intolerant, since they feel they know the "correct method" and are not supportive to any other alternative. It is important to remember rest, courage, and tolerance when confronting intolerant people.

We need to learn all virtues in life, then we will lead a happier life. To meet our tasks, we need to develop positive qualities as much as possible. However, we must recognize that negative qualities also exist. We need to learn to master these negative qualities and to transform them into positive ones. Help your child to develop positive qualities, that is the best way to fight negative characteristics. In fact, *fight* is not the right word. A better way of saying it is that on our path of development we have to learn to *transform* those things, which are not yet good.

When we performed wrong actions in a former life, then we have to transform them into positive ones in this or a future life. Therefore, we also need to make ourselves familiar with the right qualities. These are the tools, which lead to a healthier society. When as many people as possible have gained these tools, then those who are less blessed in this respect will be drawn to those who have already reached this higher level. Thus they are offered the chance to learn, see and do more positive things in life. Through this spiritual insight, you (as well as your children) will understand the stimulation of positive qualities will have a positive influence on all people.

Do not let your child get hardened by the negativity in life, for then it is the most difficult to bring forth those positive qualities. Just think about it, what effect do violent movies or video games have on your child? What does it teach your child when violence is being glorified? Faith, hope, and love will give courage and tolerance. What you emanate, your child receives and in return it can also emanate to others.

In the end, it comes down to the fact that children need to be educated correctly. Rudolf Steiner often spoke on this subject. He even provided a pedagogy for the schools. It is beyond the scope of these lessons to describe his pedagogy here. These schools (called Rudolf Steiner or Waldorf Schools) meet the possibilities of the child; so that it can develop individually, however, maintain its connection with the society. *(1)

Each child is an individual with its own possibilities. The teacher has to discover each student's possibilities and then stimulate growth of these qualities, which were brought from the Spirit world. This method focuses on the individuality of the child, instead of what happens in other schools where the child's individuality is buried under conforming to the normalcy of the masses.

Individual power is what matters. With that individual power, the child came to our planet earth. That power is meant to grow, so that the child can unfold its deeper inner being. You as a parent are supporting this process. Isn't this a beautiful task?

1)   The Education of the Child in the Light of Anthroposophy, On-line since: 23rd June 2002, By Rudolf Steiner, Bn 34.1.23; GA 34

X Learning and Story Telling
September 23, 2014

After I finish my meditation, Sita immediately begins to deliver her messages. Every day she surprises me, with much information she gives me.

Sita: Today we are going to talk about your child's learning opportunities. It has more opportunities to learn than one would think, since it learns information from everywhere.

Do not be a mother hen with her wings of protection spread over her child for the entire day. Your child needs the opportunity to explore and discover things independently, on its own. Be sure to give your child space, to allow it to be on a discovery tour of life. Let your child learn in its own unique way, provided the child will not be endangered. This way you will discover where its interest lies and what it is attracted to. Does it like to be among people or does it prefer to be on its own and be left in peace? Let it go its own way. Just keep an eye on your child from a distance. In this way, it begins to exercise autonomy at a very young age; since it is necessary that it can feel free -- free, but protected.

Today children are much more controlled than a few generations ago. Many children can't leave their home, without their parents calling them by mobile phone or sending them text messages, asking them where they are and what they are doing. This lack of privacy is greatly hindering the development of the child because it has to justify its whereabouts for the entire day. A child needs to discover its own boundaries and the world around it. Children need their own space without being continuously controlled or looked after. They should not feel their parent's fear and worry all day long. This will prevent them from learning to move freely and independently.

All senses need to be developed; therefore, plan activities that you can do with your child at home. For example, you could bake a cake or cookies together. While doing this, you can teach your child about the ingredients, and daily food in a playful easy manner. Take your child to a concert. I do not mean a pop concert with electronic instruments, but a concert with acoustic music instruments in order to allow your child to become familiar with the natural sounds.

Provide your child with a wide variety of experiences, which will expose it to a wide range of possibilities. This tour of opportunities will facilitate the child's discovery of its likes and dislikes, and will be an easy method to discover where its interest lies. Your child will gather a collection of positive impressions, which it can carry with it in "a small backpack" during its journey of life. That is what it's all about. We know life is a learning process and it is wonderful when we have the opportunity to learn as much as possible.

Encounters with other people build a very important foundation that enables the child to grow. As human beings, we can't flourish without the other people. How could a baby survive without its parents?

One often finds a deeper meaning in life during positive encounters with people. Encounters between people are what makes us human beings. We wake up through another. We grow through another. We learn life through all those other people. We hear their stories and discover how they live. Of course, this process begins within the family. Therefore, when your child has the opportunity to stay with another family, it can "perform miracles." Your child learns to move in another atmosphere, learns new habits and has the opportunity to adapt to new situations. It is important to teach your child at a young age to deal with other people in a positive way.

Stimulate the love of learning when it is possible. Stimulate your child's curiosity, but of course within limits. Also, make sure your child has time to rest and process what it has learned.

Show your child your studious nature, by reading fairy tales and constructive children's books to your child. The culture of story-telling in our society has almost disappeared. We hardly listen to the elderly. Television and the internet now occupy the dominant place within the family, replacing the wisdom of our ancestors.

Offer your child the opportunity to meet people, who have rich stories to tell. Tell your own stories to your child as well. As youngsters, we can learn much from the stories of our elders and other adults. It is important to know how one's grandfathers and grandmothers lived, especially what their lives were like, when they were younger. The life experience of previous generations is extremely different than today's experiences. Decades ago, there were no computers, television, and even supermarkets. People were more self-sufficient and grew their own food. Your child will learn there was a time when food was not found in beautiful shops nicely cut into pieces and packed in individual parcels. There were even times when the supply of food was insufficient.

Nothing is self-evident, because we do not come to this world with complete knowledge. We have to work for everything, but before we can work at something, we have to learn to work. Learning is of primary importance during our lifetime. Learning begins as soon as we take our first breath, and will not end until we take our last breath. Your child will learn this, when it comes into contact with its elders. The older generation has so much knowledge to share: stories that are real and are not fictional as is seen on television.

When you teach your children about the immortality of the soul you can use the symbol of the butterfly. During its life, the butterfly undergoes a complete change. Its life begins when it creeps out of its cocoon, and looks nothing like it did before. However, if you don't believe in immortality, then your child will not pick up on this. The story will not have the same effect, as if you believed it yourself.

Give your child the opportunity to become very acquainted with real life and wait as long as possible to bring it into contact with the virtual world. There are many harmful disadvantages to the virtual world. It diverts your child's attention away from reality: staring at a screen without purpose, without interaction, is not beneficial for the physical or mental health of your child. Furthermore, virtual games glorify many negative aspects of humanity, and will tempt your child to be more negative. It affects the soul of your child. You must think about this! It also alters the muscular movement and the eyes. In the future more will be discovered about this.

Virtual games denigrate humans into machines and only serves to enrich certain people. Virtual games replace reality and paralyse youth, preventing them from discovering their destiny -- the tasks their souls need to fulfil in their lives. The meaning of life, however, is to develop the human species into independent, thinking, feeling and willing beings.

XI The Red Thread

September 25, 2014

This morning after I finished my beautiful meditation, Sita was there, waiting for me. What will she discuss today? I had to tilt my paper a bit so I could write easier and quicker. During each session, Sita gives me so much information.

Sita: These messages are designed for parents, who want to raise their children to reach their utmost potential. In these complicated times, it is extremely important and necessary to raise your children with spiritual awareness. However, this cannot be done unless the parents themselves are spiritually aware. Still, parents can learn aspects of spirituality from their child by listening to it and by listening to inspirations originating from the Spirit world. To receive the positive inspirations from Spirit, it is extremely important that you embrace life, be independent and have good intentions. By focusing on the positive things in life, you will attract positivity in your life. This will enhance your ability to receive high-quality Spirit inspirations. Pray and have confidence. Be clear with yourself and your child. Know with clarity, what you want to achieve in life, and how you want to lead your life. Then you will be a better role model for your child, and will be totally equipped to support your child on its own journey.

If you are distracted by trivialities, they can become the central focus of your life, and then you will lose focus of your spiritual path. Then your child will follow your example and also ignore its spiritual path. After a certain point, it becomes extremely difficult to shift your focus back to the spiritual path.

So just think about how you organize your life. What burdens do you assume, which are not necessary, and keep you from your spiritual destiny? Live your life in the present. Be aware of what is happening in the world around you; however, be careful not get completely caught up in earthly matters. Always remember you also have spiritual matters that you must focus on.

Remember also human beings are NOT perfect. We are allowed to make mistakes, in fact, often our greatest learning takes place from the mistakes we made. Be honest; do your best; that is what counts. The main thing is that we strive to move forward; every human being on his/her own path. Every human has his own unique path to travel, and no one's path is better than another's.

That is also true for your child; who also will learn from mistakes, by falling and standing up again. Support it and help it, meanwhile being conscious what lies ahead in your child's development. Some paths are easier than others, who may have difficult karmic obstacles to overcome. Help each other when you can. We always are being supported by Spirit, and human support increases our stamina to travel along our journey. However, our life doesn't always go the way we like. Higher truths are sometimes hidden in life. Things happen in a certain way and it may be for a reason that we don't understand. All this belongs to the mystery of life, because we can't have all the answers. However, be assured everything has a reason: a deeper hidden cause. Our task as human beings is to deal with the mysteries of life in the best way possible. As a parent, caretaker, or teacher we have the task to coach and guide the children to the best of our ability. In return, we learn much from the children in our care. Perhaps at times we learn more from them than they learn from us. This is especially true when you are guiding a child with a physical or mental handicap.
Your path as a parent intersects your child's path, and you will walk part of your journey together, for either a long or short

period of time. This may be because there is karma between you that needs to be balanced.

We can't always know those deeper histories and truths; however, we can know with certainty, truth is behind everything. All events happen in our lives for a reason, despite the fact that we may be ignorant of what that reason is. When we understand and accept this, then we will see these events in a different light. Life will become very exciting when we learn to see that everything has a meaning. Each event has a reason. Sometimes, it may take many years until we realize the deeper meaning of a certain event. It is then that we realize what the real reason was and how it truly affected our life.

Don't limit yourself by saying: "I don't know why that happened" or "It doesn't matter." Sometimes you must feel for the deeper background. Be curious and look for it. Search for it in yourself! Life becomes more meaningful and enriched when you learn to do this.

How exciting it is when a baby comes into your life: a child that has a direct connection with you! As future parents just think about that! Two people receive a child and that child will shape their lives. When I used the term "you," I mean the parents or educators.

Why has this child come to you? It has chosen you as parents because it loves you. I repeat: it loves you! Look again and again and see how your child's love formed its connections with you and other people.

When we shine the light of karma and reincarnation on our relationships, we discover hidden worlds lying underneath the surface that are not always easily explained: love affairs, quarrels, misfortune, faith and so on. Red threads are connecting all of them creating intricate patterns. Learn to look, feel and understand these patterns. We all have a past, that is interwoven with other people's pasts. Learn to see those networks and then you will make great discoveries. You will discover how real karma and reincarnation are. These discoveries will be most helpful, and enable you to have a deeper understanding of how life works. Just think about that.

At present, you are also working at your next life on earth. From that perspective, it is beneficial to gain insight into your past, so that you see the red thread clearly.

But no matter how difficult your life may become, you must always remember, you do not live your life alone. The angels and your deceased relatives and friends, who live in the Spirit world, are always there to help you. So know without a shadow of doubt, that as you walk your path and reach out to take your child's hand, your angels are walking beside you, making you strong!

Our parents and ancestors called the supreme being "God" or "our dear Lord." They lived their lives trusting in God, who helped and supported them during difficult times. Know that our dear Lord is still watching over us, even when you are not aware of it.

I have to tell you these things, because I see how so much sorrow could be alleviated or even prevented, when people realize the presence of God, his angels and Spirit. Children are not being raised with this knowledge anymore, which creates a big void. On this beautiful earth, on this wonderful creation, mankind has come so far, yet it sees itself as a mere coincidence! A coincidence without any meaning! However, this idea is completely wrong. This philosophy where God's existence is being denied has created a void -- a huge emotional emptiness. It is now when mankind opens its eyes once again and realizes that something exists that is higher than itself. It does not matter what you call it.

This is what I wanted to say to you today: look underneath the surface, because it is there, hidden from view, you will find the ultimate richness of life. There you will find the red thread.

Finally, teach your child this simple evening prayer. When you look at it objectively, you will feel the great power of these simple words. Their effect is undeniable.

"Now the light has gone away
Saviour, listen while I pray
Asking Thee to watch and keep
And to send me quiet sleep."

XII Giving Light
September 26, 2014

I see Sita sitting in her green chair. That's a familiar image, a memory from the days when she was still alive. She is waiting for me to be ready to write.

Sita: Ria, do not feel pressure, just see whether it works. I know that when you are connected with me, you pick up my thoughts very well.

A child needs light, and it should grow up in the light. However, I am well aware this ideal situation is not possible for many children in your world. However, when it is possible, light and living without worry create the best atmosphere in which to nurture a child's growth. Then a child can freely unfold itself.

Children who are born in difficult surroundings and grow up under difficult circumstances, definitely face obstacles. However, that doesn't mean they can't overcome these obstacles. The first priority for a child is to have its basic needs of life. If parents cannot offer them to their child, or if the child is not wanted; then the child grows up under very oppressive circumstances, and has to find ways to overcome this obstacle. Of course, help is always offered from the Spirit world. However, if the parents are unfamiliar with the Spirit world, and their focus is on their daily sorrows and troubles, this help often remains unnoticed. Despite this, children sometimes feel the presence of those transcendental Spirit helpers. They consider themselves lucky not to be alone because they feel help from the Spirit world.

Everything is possible. Miracles are possible. Nothing is impossible for the world of Spirit.

Spirit help is available for every situation a person may have; even for teenagers, who frequently do rebellious things because it is their age of discovery. It will pass: it is part of the development in a human life. Yet, Spirit is still there to guide them.

Problems are like a big ball of threads that have become entangled. It takes time, attention and perseverance to unravel it all. Look at a problem in this way and teach this to your child, so that it can grow up with the skill to handle its problems. You can find red threads everywhere. After you have found it, then you have the ability to unravel the knot.

Always give hope and light. And do this repeatedly. Always remember, we don't have to cope with problems on our own. The Spirits living in the Spirit World are always there to assist us!

The world of spirit
is only a breath away,
with an answer to your questions,
with support in difficult times,
to provide light in the darkness

The German author, Dieter Lauenstein, wrote about patterns in the human course of life. The human biography is going through different stages from infancy, childhood, puberty and so on. Each stage has its own characteristics, which are more or less the same for everyone. Also, times full of problems and difficult situations are usually turning points in a person's life. They often *happen at a specific age. The so-called "moon knots" are of great importance. These are periods with a rhythm of approximately nineteen years *(1) in which life altering changes takes place. Therefore, major turning points often occur around the nineteenth year, the thirty-seventh, the fifty-sixth year and so on. Sometimes these turning points are difficult to go through, but these moments of crisis happen to everyone in one way or another. And then something happens through which the knot is unravelled.*

*From the Spirit world, Sigwart informs a mother that her child is surrounded by fears and worries. *(2)*

He says that initially, he couldn't reach the child, as the child was covered in thick layers of worries and fears. Fear creates an unclean, thick, heavy atmosphere around the child, which is difficult for Spirit to penetrate. Unless this dense atmosphere of fear dissipates, the poor child cannot develop in the proper way.

Sigwart tells the mother how to help her child. First, the mother must overcome her own fears. When the mother can freely emanate the strong feeling of love, without it being diluted by negative thoughts, then the energy of love gravitates into the child. This will dissipate the child's fear, opening the door for Spirit to help the child. Therefore, the mother should never forget that only she can help her child through her own further spiritual development. The best opportunity for this lasts until the child has reached the age of seven.

1) The exact time is 18 years, seven months and nine days.
2) Bridge over the river, http://www.sigwart.weebly.com

XIII The Sense of Truth, Beauty, and Goodness
September 27, 2014

As I sit down to begin my work, Sita is waiting for me just like yesterday. She appears very youthful and in good health. Today she feels very close to me.

Sita: Now we are going to talk about children once again. Many children are alone in life and have to cope with everything on their own. Fortunately, they have a natural compass. This compass does not point to North or South but directs them to the Spirit world. Thanks to this guidance from Spirit, they can navigate their course. This does not only apply to children, but to every human being, as well. We are NOT alone, for we all have this compass.

Let parents use it when they educate their children. It is all about choosing the right direction and the right positive path. That path that will lead you to the light. When we walk along the right path, nothing can happen to us, however, that does not mean we won't meet difficulties along the way. Nevertheless, the path leads to the ultimate purpose: to become absorbed in the world of light. Then in your next incarnation you will be able to work further on the development of humanity. We live eternally.

It is crucial for our future and our future afterlife, to choose the right direction. Of course, we cannot think about this the entire day. But just remember that it is important that we as human beings should do our best to do good. You have such a beautiful saying on the façade of your house.

67

This saying was written on my house in Switzerland in 1921: "Das Wahre suchen, das Schöne lieben, das Gute üben, kein reiner Glück kann auf Erden den Menschen werden." (Searching for the truth, loving the beautiful, practising the good, no purer happiness can happen to men on earth.)

Just think about this saying, for it contains the blueprint for a happy life. It seems so simple, but it can take a long time to accomplish. Our life is like a labyrinth, where we confront many winding roads and our path intersects with wrong paths along our way. However, with the correct attitude we can travel along the right path. Use the saying written on your house, as your compass to lead you along your life's path.

What is the beautiful? It is something spiritual that appears in matter. Think of the rose. We often see the rose as a symbol of love.

What is the truth? The truth is that which guides us on our path to the horizon, where the great divine light shines that waits for us.

What is the good? The good is that which makes our heart beat quietly in our chest. It inspires us with courage to continue in life. Then when evening comes we can directly look at ourselves in the mirror, without casting our eyes down in shame.

When we try to live our lives in this manner, we become full of happiness and gratitude.

Today our focus seems to be on ourselves, instead of our children. However, today's message is the core of all you can give to your children. Teach them insight into truth, beauty, and goodness. Those are the road signs on our path of life, which show us the right direction. Other signs lead away from that path into the desert and the darkness. I do not have to explain to you what we can find there. We can see that on the news and in our streets. It is not far away from us.

Never feel superior to those who have dropped their compass, and have lost their way along their path of life. It is very tempting to explore paths that take you in the wrong direction. However, once that path is explored, it is not always easy to find the way back. Rejection makes it even more difficult for people to return to their "right path."

Many people carry a backpack as they walk along their life's journey. These backpacks contain problems. Some backpacks are small, and some are large. Some contain problems from the person's youth and some problems from former lives.

Of course, the specific issues contained in the backpack is not as important as learning to address and deal with these problems. Do you really want to carry that burden for your entire life's journey? Wouldn't you find it easier to deal with the problem, so it comes out of your backpack? Then you could continue your journey without carrying the weight of that problem.

Think about this again and again. Then you will not only know the best course for yourself, but also you will become the best example for your child.

In the first Chapter we started with Sita's poem "The Guardian Angel". I finish here with this poem, as it summarizes the content of the book. After reading this book I hope you see your child in a different light.

The Guardian Angel

I knew you before you came

freshly born as a child to the earth.

I took your hand and helped you stand

and go the long way we call life.

And know I shall not leave you,

even not when all is done.

We go together on a path

of stumbling and standing up.

In God's name once we will

overcome all that is difficult.

After much love and grief

We enter heaven together.

The original Dutch text is as follows:

De Beschermengel

Ik kende je al voordat je als kindje

vers geboren op de aarde kwam.

Ik nam je hand en hielp je staan

en gaan de lange weg die leven heet.

En weet ik zal je niet verlaten,

ook niet al is het al gedaan.

We gaan tezaam

een weg van vallen en van opstaan

en weer verder gaan.

In Godes naam zullen we

al wat moeilijk is eens overwinnen.

We trekken na veel lief en leed

samen de hemel binnen.

Epilogue

One should not accept the messages from the Spirit world on blind faith, but should judge or consider if the message resonates with one's own soul. This is true for both messages from the deceased as well as messages from the spiritual beings, which can be found in many books today. The person must consider the communicator of these messages. Messages claiming to be from the archangel Michael or Jesus can come from another source. These messages also need to be translated into our language without being coloured by the ideas and emotions of the receivers. Therefore, readers cannot accept the content of these messages without considering whether the content of the messages feels significant and valid.

In this book, there is a reference to the messages of the deceased Botho Sigwart von Eulenburg (1884-1915), which were received by his sister Lycki and other family members. The English translation titled: Bridge over the River was published in 2008, and can be found on the website: http://sigwart.weebly.com/. When Rudolf Steiner, who was considered a specialist in these matters, first read these messages, he said: "These are extremely clear, [and are] absolute authentic messages from the Spirit world. I do not see any reason to dissuade you from listening to them." Then he remarked, "such messages are very rare."

Over a period of several years, Rudolf Steiner received messages from Helmuth von Moltke after Moltke's death in 1916. Steiner passed these messages on to Moltke's widow. These messages were first published in 1993. For the English translation, see: Thomas Meyer (editor), Helmuth von Moltke, Light for the New Millennium: Rudolf Steiner's association with

Helmuth and Eliza von Moltke, Rudolf Steiner Press, London, 1997.

Sita ten Cate, the "communicator" of this book's messages, was familiar with Rudolf Steiner's work. In this book, she speaks as a friendly, wise woman, who is concerned about the circumstances in which modern children grow up and therefore wants to give well-meaning advice for their parents. Her advice about all kinds of relevant aspects of modern education actualizes what Rudolf Steiner said a century ago about how to educate children. His theories have become the foundation for the Steiner schools.

Harrie Salman Ph.D.

Bibliography

• Prayers for Mothers and Children, Rudolf Steiner
http://wn.rsarchive.org/Articles/Prayers/Prayrs_a01.html

• Bridge over the river, Translated by Joseph Wetzel, Steiner Books 1974, ISBN 9780910142595

• How Does One Attain Knowledge of Higher Worlds? Rudolf Steiner, GA 10

• The Mission of the Archangel Michael, The Revelation of the Secrets of Mans Being, By Rudolf Steiner, lecture December 6, 1919 in Dornach, Bn 194.1 and 174a, GA 194 and 174a (English text published in the Golden Blade, 1984)

• The Spiritual Hierarchies and their Reflection in the Physical World. Zodiac, Planets and Cosmos (GA 110)

• Death is of Vital Importance, Elisabeth Kübler-Ross, Station Hill Press, Barrytown, New York, USA, 1995

• The Education of the Child in the Light of Anthroposophy, On-line since: 23rd June 2002, By Rudolf Steiner, Bn 34.1.23; GA 34, Translated by George and Mary Adams.

• The Lucifer-Gnosis: Foundational Essays on Anthroposophy and Reports from the Periodical 'Lucifer-Gnosis' 1903-1908 GA 34

Manufactured by Amazon.ca
Acheson, AB

12511809R00044